My First Book of Nautical Knots

A GUIDE TO SAILING AND DECORATIVE KNOTS

by Caroline Britz
Illustrated by Laura Gómez Guerra
Translated by Andrea Jones Berasaluce

Sky Pony Press
New York

TABLE OF CONTENTS

Guidelines and Materials   4

The Benefits of Ropework   5

Slip Knot   7
Creating Adjustable Jewelry Using a Slip Knot   9

Figure Eight Knot   11
Making a Pretty Bracelet Using a Figure Eight Knot   13

Bowline   14

Round Turn and Two Half Hitches   16

Overhand Knot   18

Cleat   20

Clove Hitch   22

Heaving Line Knot   24

Carrick Bend   27
Making a Bracelet Using a Carrick Bend   29

Fisherman's Knot   **30**

Thump Mat   **32**
Making a Little Rug Using a Thump Mat   35

Love Knot   **37**
Love Knots for Hanging Small Objects or
Making a Bracelet   39

Diamond Knot   **40**
Making a Key Ring with a Diamond Knot   43

Celtic Heart Knot   **45**
Making Jewelry with a Celtic Heart Knot   47

Sailor's Cross Knot   **49**
Making Sailor's Cross Knot Jewelry   51

Monkey Fist   **52**

Bonus! Gimp Stitching   **57**

Your Table of Knots   **62**

GUIDELINES AND MATERIALS

Do you know what ropework is ? It's the art of knowing how to make knots! Aboard sailing vessels many types of knots exist, all of them different. Some are used to raise sails, others to lengthen ropes; some are tied in the blink of an eye, others require greater concentration. And some are even so pretty that you can use them to make a necklace or to propose to your beloved …

Sailors have perfected the art of tying knots and passed on this knowledge from generation to generation. And today, young sailor, you will learn how to tie these knots. All you'll need to do is have some materials ready, and follow the instructions step by step.

To make these knots, you can use any kind of thread, string, or rope. You can start practicing with cooking twine or laces. The key is to have strands long enough that you can complete the knot. To make bracelets, you can use cotton or elastic threads if you want to add beads or small charms. Of course, for gimp stitching, you'll need plastic lacing. You'll find all these supplies—in various colors and with different diameters—in a haberdashery or a hobby/ crafts store.

Once you become a seasoned sailor, you can try to tie knots with ropes made of textile, hemp, or synthetic fiber. This kind of rope is sold in stores specializing in sports equipment, do-it-yourself, or at maritime cooperatives.

THE BENEFiTS OF ROPEVVORK

To learn to make a knot, you'll have to be methodical and always pay attention to the direction in which you're making a loop or whether you're passing one strand under or over another. You must respect each step and keep calm. You'll see your concentration greatly improve thanks to making knots!

Once you've memorized the different steps for a knot, you'll find you can make it more and more quickly, and maybe even with just one hand, like the old salts. Your fingers will become more and more agile!

But that's not all. Getting the knots down will enable you to make many objects: key chains, bracelets and necklaces, pendants, small rugs. … Let your imagination and creativity run free.

Some Vocabulary

First things first, you need to know some essential words in order to make knots. A knot consists of two or more strands.

The strand that you move, with which you make loops or turns, it's called the **running end**. The strand that's not moving is called the **standing end**. When we talk about firmly tightening a knot, we sometimes call that making something fast!

SLIP KNOT

Here we have a very simple, very effective, and very handy knot! It will be really useful for all the jewelry that you'll discover how to make in this book.

What's it for?

It's mainly for tightening a thread or rope around an object. The more you pull it, the more it tightens. It's therefore used to hang things or to attach objects such as carabiners.

But it can also be a decorative knot. For those who like to crochet, it's also very useful to make in the yarn as a start to a length of slip stitches.

stern lines

spring lines

Did you know?

The slip knot is also used for the hangman's knot. At sea, we never say the word *rope* itself because a rope was used to hang mutineers. This is why sailors invented many different words for ropes on boats and ships: ends, shrouds, sheets, halyards, hawsers, stern lines, spring lines … but never ropes!

Making a Slip Knot

1 Make a loop.

2 Make sure the middle of the standing end passes through the loop.

3 Tighten the loop and your standing end. You can add a simple knot, like the kind on your shoelaces, at the end of your running end. The knot is finished!

Creating Adjustable Jewelry Using a Slip Knot

It's useful to have necklaces or bracelets that can get longer and shorter when you want to swap jewelry with friends. Thanks to the slip knot, you can adjust the length of your creations however you like. You can also, for example, slide pearls or small charms onto a little cord or thread and then close with a slip knot.

FIGURE EIGHT KNOT

This is one of the easiest knots to tie and untie, and, without a doubt, one of the most useful!

What's it for?

It's a stopper knot: placed at the end of a rope or line to prevent it from escaping the hole in which it has gone. We also use the figure eight knot to make knots for climbing ropes! It's strong enough that it can hold your weight.

Once you know how to make it, you can use this knot on a boat, at the end of the sheets that position the sails. And most importantly, every morning to tie your shoelaces!

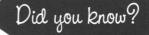
Did you know?

In ancient times, builders made thirteen figure eight knots, all the same distance from each other along a long rope. Thanks to this, they could measure heights or draw geometric shapes. A little like a tape measure!

Making a Figure Eight Knot

To do this, you just have to make an eight.

 Grab the running end and pass it under the standing end to form a loop.

 Take the running end and go back over the standing end.

 Thread it through the first loop.

Pull the strands, and your figure eight knot is made fast (tightened)!

Making a Pretty Bracelet Using a Figure Eight Knot

It's easy! Choose a rope or thread made from plastic or textile. Calculate the length needed to go around your wrist. Find the middle of your cord, and make your figure eight knot there. You can choose to tighten it firmly or, if your thread is thick, leave it a little slack. You can then close your bracelet with whatever knot or clasp you like.

BOWLINE

This is the knot that all sailors, professional or recreational, absolutely must know! It's very easy to tie and untie.

What's it for?

At sea, it's for connecting the sheets—the sails' lines. One of its features is that it doesn't tighten even when subjected to very strong strains and tensions. And when holding back a huge sail beating in the wind, the knot can still be undone very quickly, which is very important in case of an emergency on board.

Though the front of the ship is called the bow, this is not related to the origin of the word bowline. And if you were to use big enough ropes, you could even sit in the loop of a bowline.

Did you know?

The bowline is so useful and necessary that it's one of the first knots you learn how to make aboard a ship. To be sure that everyone, adults as well as kids, remembers how to tie it, there's a little story that explains the steps. In the story, the rope is a snake that comes out of a hole, goes around the tree, and then goes back down into the hole. It's a very useful way to remember how to make the knot!

Making a Bowline

Feel free to imagine the rabbit and the rabbit hole!

 1 Take the standing end in your left hand. With your right hand, make a loop above the standing end—*that's your rabbit hole.*

 2 Put the running end through the loop— *the rabbit comes out of the rabbit hole.*

3 Pass it under the standing end—*the rabbit goes behind the tree.*

4 Then put it back through the loop—*the rabbit returns to its rabbit hole.*

5 Tighten the knot by pulling on both the running and standing ends.

ROUND TURN AND TWO HALF HITCHES

If you're going to learn just one nautical knot, this is it! And it so happens that it's very easy to tie and also very solid.

What's it for?

The knot called "round turn and two half hitches" serves a lot of purposes on a boat, but it's mainly for attaching objects.

It's useful because you can tie and untie it very quickly, and it even works on very tense ropes.

Did you know?

Sailors have always liked proverbs and sayings. They have a lot of seagoing phrases. It's not that sailors are chatterboxes, rather it's a way to learn and also pass on their knowledge to younger crew members.

For example, a well-known sailors' expression in French is "Reeving a round turn and two half hitches never fails." *Reeve* is a nautical word that refers to putting a rope through an opening, such as a ring. Since the dawn of time sailors have known that this knot is solid, and that's why they came up with that saying.

Making a Round Turn and Two Half Hitches

 Make a loop all the way around the object to which you want to attach the rope—*this is the round turn.*

 Make a simple knot by passing the running end over and then under the standing end—*this is the first half hitch.*

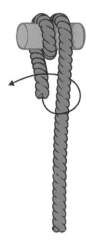

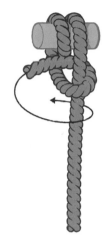

 Do the exact same thing again, i.e. make a simple knot just below the first one—*this is the second half hitch.*

 Pull on both rope ends to tighten.

OVERHAND KNOT

The sea and the mountain seem worlds apart. Yet many knots used by sailors are also used by mountaineers.

What's it for?

You can use the overhand knot to make a loop at the end of a rope. This knot serves to attach things together or, more commonly, to lengthen a rope.

You can use it to extend lines, but you should know that it's not an easy knot to loosen!

Did you know?

In mountaineering, when climbers are facing a steep wall, they use a rope to climb up and hold them in case they fall. Climbers attach themselves to the rope with harnesses, while mountaineers do so using carabiners. They use a technique called belaying, and the overhand knot is very practical then!

In some countries, this knot is known by other funny names. This knot is sometimes called the granny knot or the lubber's knot.

Making an Overhand Knot

 Take a doubled section of rope and make a loop by going under the standing end with both strands at the same time.

 Go back through the inside of the first loop with the double strands. You have now formed a solid loop that can serve to attach to another rope or object.

 Pull the end firmly to tighten the knot.

CLEAT

This is a very useful knot aboard a boat, since it can be tied even when the rope is taut. It is also very easy to undo: handy if you have to leave the dock very quickly!

What's it for?

It is very important to moor (attach) a boat securely when at a dock.

Whether it's a very small sailboat or a very large tanker, the moorings are there to prevent it from being carried away by the current and wind. The bigger the boat, the more moorings. For recreational boats, the cleat knot is used to securely attach the boat to the dock. It is also used on boat decks for all ropes that must be kept securely.

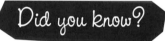
Did you know?

A cleat is a very flat and long T made of metal or wood. Around it we form the cleat knot. But for larger boats, other types of equipment are used: these can be very large rings or mooring bollards, which are very large cylinders of wood or steel affixed to the dock. In general, a boat must be moored with lines that attach to it at the fore and aft, as well as lines that prevent it from moving forward and backward.

Making a Cleat

1. Go once around the cleat with the rope.

2. Cross your strand, then go around the cleat horn. Bring the running end back over your standing end.

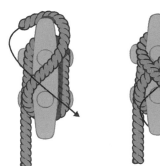

3. With the running end, make a loop, then invert it.

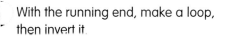

4. Stick your inverted loop on the other horn of the cleat.

CLOVE HITCH

You can see clove hitches on recreational boats moored along docks. This easy-to-make knot is very practical for use at home.

What's it for?

Sometimes on a boat, you must quickly attach an object or a line. For example, when you come near a dock, you must quickly put down the fenders—the big buoys that protect the hull and prevent it from rubbing against the dock. To do so, sailors use a not-so-solid knot that's very easy to tie, so much so that it can be tied with one hand.

Did you know?

The clove hitch, along with the capstan formerly, is an important part of mooring and departing. The capstan was, aboard a boat, the machine used to raise the anchor or to maneuver anything heavy. In the past, the sailors had to turn a big wheel around, which a cable was wound to raise the anchor. Nowadays, we use a machine called a winch. And though both were used for mooring, you never tie the clove hitch to the capstan!

Making a Clove Hitch Using Mickey Mouse Ears

One of the many techniques for making a clove hitch and, no doubt, the funniest one, uses Mickey Mouse's ears.

 1 Form two loops with your line. Separate them to shape them into Mickey Mouse ears.

 2 Make them overlap.

3 Your knot is finished.

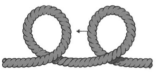

Alternative

 1 Make a first loop around your support. Pass the running end over your standing end.

 2 Make a second loop next to the first loop.

3 Slide the running end under the second loop. Firmly tighten the knot.

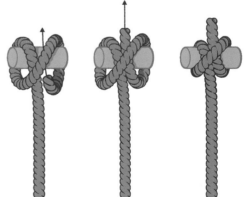

HEAVING LINE KNOT

The heaving line knot is also called the Franciscan monk's knot. It's amusing with its corkscrew-like appearance.

What's it for?

It's a knot used to weigh down the ends of ropes and keep them from escaping from their holes.

On a boat, it is often used on large ropes that are not handled very often and require a solid stopper knot.

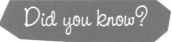
Did you know?

This knot was invented by monks. They used to tie this knot at the end of their rope belt so that it would be heavy and fall nicely. The specific order of monks is Capuchin, an offshoot of the Franciscans.

Making a Heaving Line Knot

 Grab the running end and pass it over the standing end to form a loop. Wrap the running end around the standing end inside the loop. You can wrap it around once or many times, but be sure to avoid overlapping.

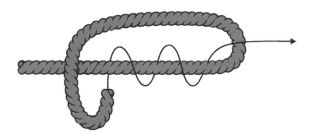

 After the last wrap, take the running end back out of the loop.

 Pull gently on the two ends of the strand.

Be aware that after five wraps, the knot will be hard to close!

CARRICK BEND

Not only is it strong, it's also very pretty. That's why it is used to plait bracelets.

What's it for?

How do you connect two pieces of rope or even a broken lace? The carrick bend can help! Sailors call it the "adding knot" in French, as it is used to lengthen a rope. The carrick bend is most useful for tying together two ropes of different sizes, which is needed quite often on a boat. But it can also help you out at home!

Did you know?

The carrick bend is very old. It dates back to the time of the first sailing ships setting out to explore the world. Among the first boats to go exploring were the carracks. Appearing at the end of the Middle Ages, these ships, about a hundred feet long each, went to cross oceans and discover new lands. It may be that we get the name of the carrick bend from them.

Making a Carrick Bend

 Form a loop with your first thread. Intertwine a second line to form a loop inside the first loop.

 You should have two loops intertwined symmetrically, one inside the other.

 To tighten, pull on the two opposite free strands.

Making a Bracelet Using a Carrick Bend

The carrick bend is a pretty pattern that can be easily used to create a bracelet. The simplest approach is to use small ropes or even laces. Take care to leave enough thread on either side of the knot so it's long enough to go around the wrist.

You can make one simple knot or several ones, repeating the technique. To make a thick knot, you can follow these same instructions, but double the strands. Once you've finished your knots, tighten them well. You can then fasten your bracelet with a slip knot or using whatever clasp you like.

FISHERMAN'S KNOT

Let's go fishing! Fishermen are great specialists in nautical knots. One knot in particular is used to tie the fishing hook.

What's it for?

Have you ever made a fishing rod using a large branch and very strong line? Or maybe you've used a real fishing rod with a reel before? In any case, when fishing, you always use a hook, which serves to attract and catch fish. To connect a hook to the end of the line, you have to tie a strong enough fisherman's knot to handle the weight of the fish, which can sometimes pull very hard in the water!

Did you know?

There are many techniques for fishing. You can use a fishing rod and hooks, of course, but you can also use a landing net to go fishing in puddles and shallow waters. You can place small nets in the currents in which the fish move. But the most beautiful technique is, without a doubt, fly fishing. To attract fish, you use colorful baits made with feathers. Then, the fisherman must make his bait jump on the water, like a fly or a dragonfly!

Making a Fisherman's Knot to Tie on a Small Object

▶ Put your line through the ring of a small object.

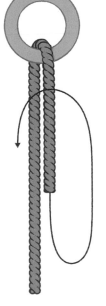

2 Go around the two standing ends several times.

▶ Put your running end back through the loop made during the first wrap.

4 Pull firmly on the object at the same time as the wire to tighten your knot.

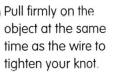

THUMP MAT

Look at this beautiful knot with which we can make all kinds of useful creations for the house!

What's it for?

A thump mat is a flat knot composed of several strands that intertwine and form a kind of small carpet.

Aboard ships, sailors use it to protect wooden parts like masts or decks from the friction caused by metal objects, especially the pulleys in the rigging. To make a thump mat, they use leftover ropes. Nothing goes to waste on a ship!

Did you know?

Thump mats can be used to make a lot of things: trivets, doormats, or even pretty pendants. It's essential to choose the rope you want based on what you plan to make: cotton or hemp to resist heat, a big rope for outdoor carpets, or elastic thread for jewelry.

Making a Thump Mat

There are a lot of loops in a thump mat, so follow the diagrams and take care to pass the running end either above or below the loops as indicated. This knot will require a little patience, but the result is so pretty that it's worth it.

Grab the running end and pass it beneath the standing end to form a loop.

 Make a second loop with the running end, going over and under the first one.

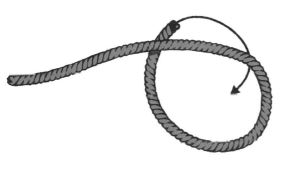

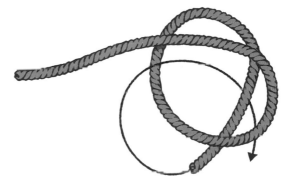

Make a third loop below the second, then pass the running end under the first loop.

 Using the running end, go over the third loop then under the standing end.

Repeat the motions, passing the running end once above and once below each loop.

 Once you've made three loops, go back to the starting point and retrace your steps to double the strand.

 Finish by going through a third time, always following the same steps.

Making a Little Rug Using a Thump Mat

The thump mat lets you make small rugs that you can, for example, slide under glasses or hot mugs or a small flowerpot. To do so, use whatever ropes you like, making sure they are water resistant if you plan to use them in the kitchen. You can choose to tighten your knot fully or leave it a little loose.

If you're brave, you can choose a rope with a larger diameter and make a real carpet, which will have the most beautiful effect in front of your bedroom door!

LOVE KNOT

This knot has a nice name and is easy to tie. Also, it allows you to make lots of jewelry.

What's it for?

It can be used to hang objects or hold pendants as well as a pattern for bracelets.

Aboard a boat, this is the knot used to hang small items or to keep a whistle around your neck.

Did you know?

The two half-knots that form it intertwine and resemble a heart, which is why sailors called it the love knot. It's even said that American whaling captains asked for the hand of their beloved by offering her a piece of rope with a love knot.

Making a Love Knot

1 Make a loop, then put the running end through it.

2 Make a simple knot on one of the two strands, but don't tighten it.

3 Put the running end through your first knot.

4 On the second strand, make a knot with your running end.

5 Pull the two strands to tighten your knot.

Love Knots for Hanging Small Objects or Making a Bracelet

A whistle around your neck, a nice pendant or keys … the love knot lets you hang, tie, or suspend anything. If you want to make a necklace, make sure that after tying the knot, the cord will still be long enough to go around your neck. Have ready the object you want to tie on, and pass it through the loop of your knot. You must then tighten firmly before attaching a fastener or a knot to close your necklace.

You can also make a key ring with the love knot: just slip a metal ring into the loop of your knot.

To make a bracelet, simply make another love knot a little farther down the strand and repeat as desired.

DIAMOND KNOT

Here is a knot that's used more for decoration than aboard boats. This beautiful knot is also called the knife lanyard knot.

What's it for?

It can be used to make key rings, necklaces, or bracelets: its pattern is so pretty!

On boats, it is sometimes used to make a "knob" that can serve as a stopper knot at the end of a rope.

Did you know?

On a boat, the quartermaster is in charge of signals and steering. It's the quartermaster who directs the maneuvering of the sails and, so that everyone knows what to do, the quartermaster uses a whistle to set the pace. With his whistle, he also greets senior officers who get on and off the boat.

Making a Diamond Knot

 Take a rope, wrap it around two of your fingers, and make a loop.

 Put the standing end back under your loop.

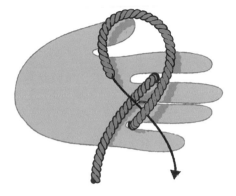

 Then form a loop.

 Pass the running end under the two loops of the standing end.

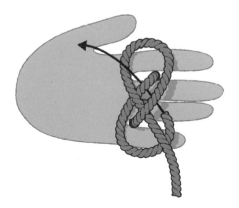

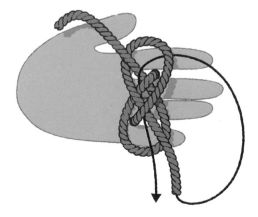

Take the standing end and bring it out through the middle of your loops.

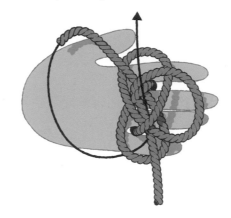

 Do the same with the running end.

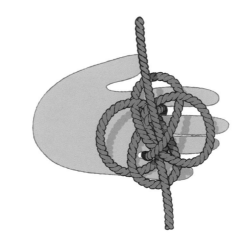

 Gently tighten the knots to form the knob.

Making a Key Ring with a Diamond Knot

The diamond knot is very handy for tying on objects. It can also be used as a key chain that can be found easily at the bottom of a bag, thanks to its big knob shape. To make one, you'll need a metal ring to hold the keys. You can put the ring through the loop of your diamond knot. To make this knot, you can use rope or string of any size and type, though the more solid, the better.

CELTIC HEART KNOT

Despite its name, this knot does not come from boats. The Celtic heart knot is one of the most beautiful and easiest knots to tie.

What's it for?

It can be used to create jewelry, headbands, or small decorative items. This design can also be easily made when working with macramé, wool, or even plastic threads.

Did you know?

The Celts are the ancestors of a large part of Western European peoples. Arriving more than three thousand years ago from Asia, they settled on a very vast territory corresponding to Great Britain, Ireland, France, and Spain. Their descendants continue to keep this culture alive, notably through the Celtic languages such as Breton or Gaelic and through traditional music featuring flutes, harps, or bagpipes.

Making a Celtic Heart Knot

1 Form a loop with your thread. Put the running end through the loop.

2 Put your running end back under the standing end and then over the first loop.

3 Take your running end back up, passing it under the first loop (1), over the standing end (2), under the loop (3), and then over the last strand.

4 Your knot is finished.

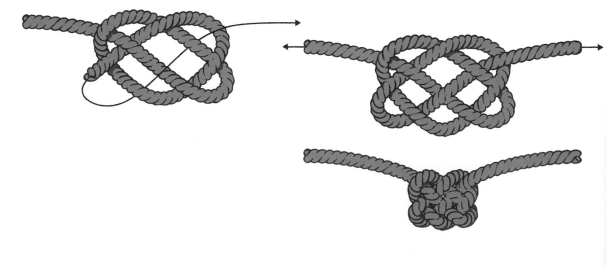

Making Jewelry with a Celtic Heart Knot

This is a nice heart to offer to those you love! The Celtic heart knot can be a motif for a bracelet or pendant. Choose a textile rope or cord that's not too thick—should you want to make a necklace, calculate the length needed to go around your wrist or your neck—find the middle of your rope, and make your knot in this spot. You can make a simple knot, but you can also tie one, for example, using two different colored threads.

This knot is called a sailor's cross, but isn't it shaped more like a clover? That's what you might notice with this knot, which is more for decoration than used on ships today.

What's it for?

It is indeed tough to tighten and does not really have any practical use on ships of late.

But it has other upsides! Its pretty shape allows for making small jewels, like pendants. It is also a classic in knot charts.

Did you know?

The sailor's cross knot takes its name from the Southern Cross constellation. These stars, which we see in the planet's southern hemisphere, are well-known to sailors. It is thanks to them that navigators could find their bearings in the southern seas. The Southern Cross is so important that the stars that comprise it are found on several national flags, like Brazil's, Australia's, and New Zealand's.

Making a Sailor's Cross Knot

1 Make a figure eight knot and put the running end through it.

2 Pass the thread through your loop and then form a new loop. The two loops should be interlaced, but don't pull on them.

3 Pull the inner two strands of the loops underneath where the outer strands cross. You now have three loops, one at the top and one on each side.

4 Gently pull on each loop and on the strands to close the middle knot.

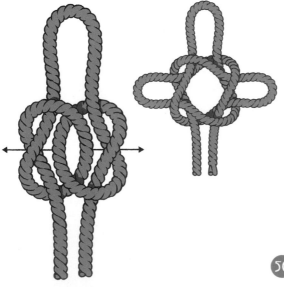

Making Sailor's Cross Knot Jewelry

It's such a pretty knot that it can easily become jewelry, such as a pendant or a fancy bracelet. Choose a rope that's a little rigid so the loops of your knot hold well. Calculate the length needed for the jewel you want to make, find the middle of your thread, and tie the knot here. Be careful to tighten only the middle knot by spreading out the loops.

MONKEY FIST

It is one of the most beautiful knots, but perhaps also one of the least easy to make.

What's it for?

The monkey fist is a round knot first created to serve as ballast or, in other words, weight, at the end of a rope that people wanted to throw onto the dock or to someone.

But it is so beautiful that sailors soon began using it as a decoration. It can also make a very nice key chain. It is sometimes plaited around a ball or a small round stone. But you should know that, for sailors traditionally, the monkey fist was only made of rope!

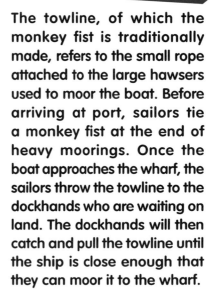

The towline, of which the monkey fist is traditionally made, refers to the small rope attached to the large hawsers used to moor the boat. Before arriving at port, sailors tie a monkey fist at the end of heavy moorings. Once the boat approaches the wharf, the sailors throw the towline to the dockhands who are waiting on land. The dockhands will then catch and pull the towline until the ship is close enough that they can moor it to the wharf.

Making a Monkey Fist

 Hold your hand vertically and make three loops around your fingers.

 Then make another three loops, perpendicular to the first three. If you want to insert a ball or a small stone, do so now.

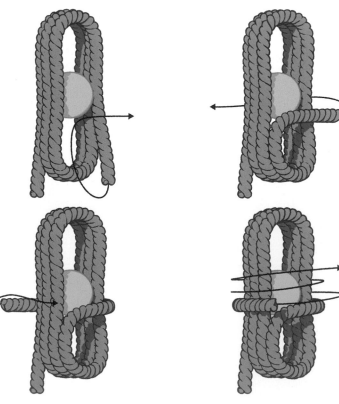

Now make three turns around the last three loops that you made (and therefore inside the first three).

 Tighten each strand carefully, making sure to pull each with the same force.

BONUS!
GIMP STITCHING

These knots don't come from the nautical world, but have become some of the most famous styles!

What's it for?

Gimp stitching has been, for years, the star on playgrounds. With plastic threads of all colors, you can braid and make key chains, bracelets, and many other colorful objects. With three, four, five threads, you can do circle stitches, square stitches, or even diagonal stitches; the possibilities are endless. Just slip some threads in your pocket, and you can stitch gimp everywhere you go!

Did you know?

Gimp stitching techniques are very old but only became something for children about sixty years ago. Its inventors came up with the idea of using plastic material to insulate electrical wires, so they made these small, flexible, and multicolored wires. And since then, children have begun to use them.

Square Stitch

 Take two same-sized strands of gimp, two different colors (orange and blue shown here), hold them parallel to each other, and bend them in the middle.

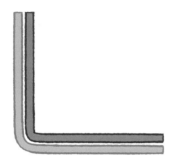

2 Make a knot in the middle and form a loop through which you can stick your finger.

3 Make an X with the gimp threads.

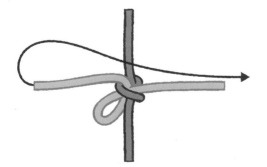

4 Take an orange strand and make one loop above the X and another below.

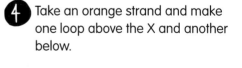

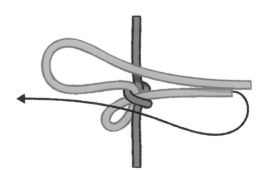

Take the blue strand and pass it through the bottom orange loop.

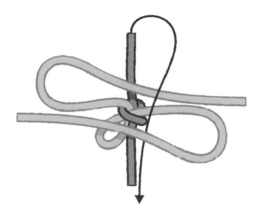

6 Take the blue strand from the bottom and put it through the top orange loop.

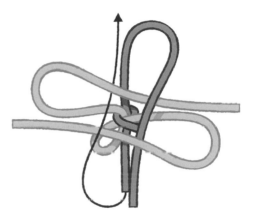

Pull all four strands at the same time.

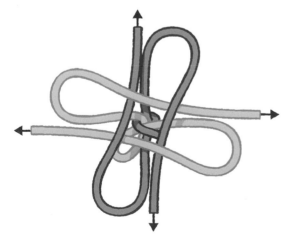

8 You have your first square stitch. Start again and keep stitching until you don't have any strand left.

Circle Stitch

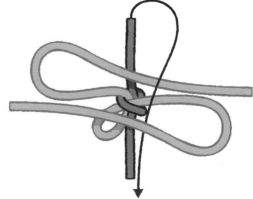

 Take two same-sized strands of gimp, two different colors (orange and blue shown here), hold them parallel to each other, and bend them in the middle.

 Make a knot in the middle to have four same-sized strands.

 Take the orange strand and make one loop above the X and another below.

Take the top blue thread and pass it through the bottom orange loop.

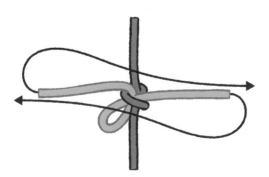

 5 Pass the bottom blue strand through the top orange loop.

6 Pull all four strands at the same time. You have your first square stitch.

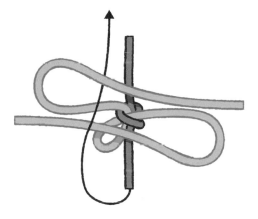

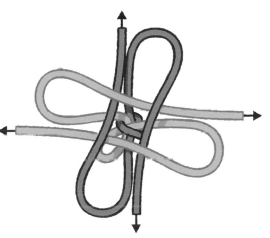

Shift your square to become a rhombus.

8 Take one strand and pull it diagonally to go back into the square at a point of the other color. Repeat with each strand.

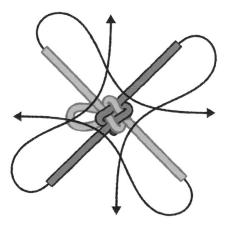

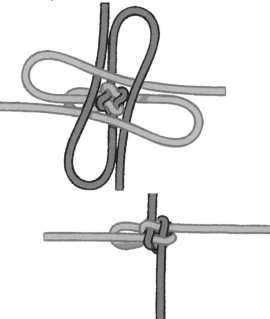

Start again and keep stitching until you don't have any gimp left.

YOUR TABLE OF KNOTS

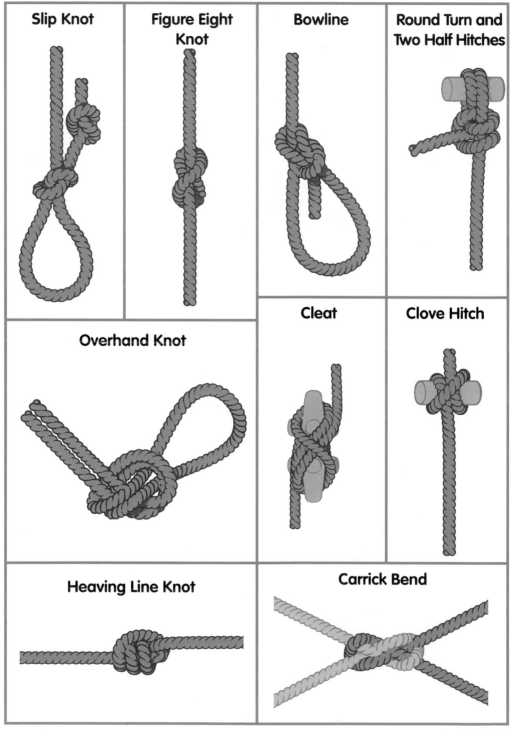

Slip Knot	Figure Eight Knot	Bowline	Round Turn and Two Half Hitches

Overhand Knot

Cleat	Clove Hitch

Heaving Line Knot

Carrick Bend

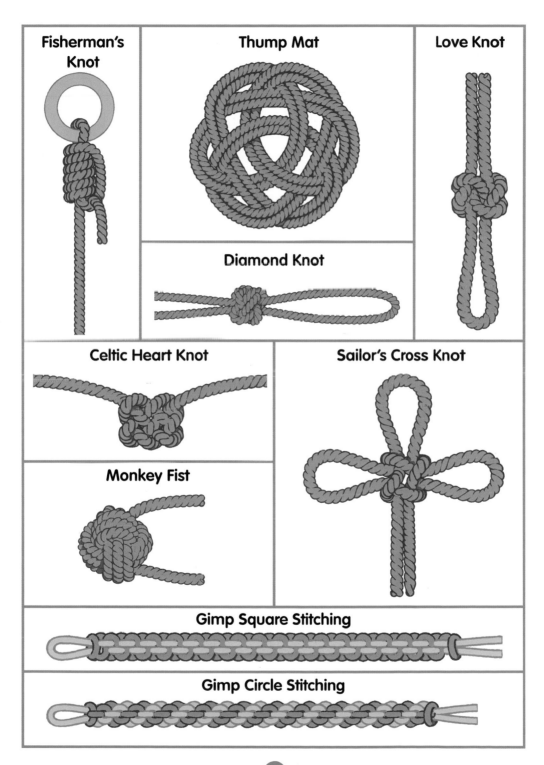

Fisherman's Knot

Thump Mat

Love Knot

Diamond Knot

Celtic Heart Knot

Sailor's Cross Knot

Monkey Fist

Gimp Square Stitching

Gimp Circle Stitching

Direction: Guillaume Pô
Editorial Direction: Élisabeth Pegeon
Editing: Sandrine Vincent
Artistic Direction: Isabelle Mayer
Illustrations: Laura Gómez Guerra
Production Management: Thierry Dubus
Manufacturing Monitoring: Marie Guibert
Translation: Andrea Jones Berasaluce

Sky Pony Press books may be purchased in bulk at special discounts for sales promotion, corporate gifts, fund-raising, or educational purposes. Special editions can also be created to specifications. For details, contact the Special Sales Department, Sky Pony Press, 307 West 36th Street, 11th Floor, New York, NY 10018 or info@skyhorsepublishing.com.

Sky Pony® is a registered trademark of Skyhorse Publishing, Inc.®, a Delaware corporation.

Visit our website at www.skyponypress.com.

10 9 8 7 6 5 4 3 2 1

Library of Congress Cataloging-in-Publication Data is available on file.

Cover Illustration by Laura Gómez Guerra
Cover design by Kai Texel

Print ISBN: 978-1-5107-5932-9
Ebook ISBN: 978-1-5107-5933-6

Printed in China